To Build a Home

To Build a Home

1

Michael Tavon

**<u>Other Works by The Author</u>**

Nirvana: Pieces of Self-Healing vol. 1 & 2
Don't Wait til I Die to Love Me vol. 1,2, & 3
Dreaming in a Perfect World
God is a Woman (Novel)
Far From Heaven (Novel)
Dreaming in a Perfect World
Before I Die, I Must Say This
Young Heart, Old Soul
Heal, Inspire, Love
Self-Talks

To Build a Home

**Social Media**

Twitter: MichaelTavon

IG: bymichaeltavon

Tiktok: MichaelTavonpoetry

Michael Tavon

Note to the Reader:

This collection is compiled of mostly new poems with the addition of poems from my previous collections. So, if you're familiar with my work, you'll probably recognize them, and if this is your first time reading one of my books, I hope you enjoy it.

# To Build

Michael Tavon

## In Search Of...

You've spent a lifetime searching for love in homes that
never welcome your light. You constantly try to break
through walls that were created to push you away. You
allow others to make a home out of you rent-free because
your heart falls so hard you believe everyone you love will
protect your heart from breaking. When they inevitably
pack their coat and never return, you rush to find the next
resident to fill the vacancy. Your fear of being alone has
created a place in your heart that only feels worthy when
someone decides to visit for small pockets of time. You
have yet to realize you already possess all the love you
need. Be your own home. Appreciate the blissful space that
resides inside you. Find solace in solitude.

## To Build a Home

Home is a collection
Of every beautiful thing
you fall in love with along the way.

As life goes on,
Those precious moments
Will be the stones
You'll build your home with

So when heaven calls
You'll have a happy place to run to

Michael Tavon

## Stratus I

When the clouds clear
And the pasture dries.

greener grass
And a brighter sky
Will shine

When the clouds clear
And the grey fog leaves.

Rearview memories
Turn faint,
No more grief

When the clouds clear
Of pouring cold sorrow

The warm
sunrise will kiss you
Tomorrow

## Stratus II

I built a house
Out of broken pieces

      Fragments turned whole
        My heart is where peace is

It took a long time
To right my wrongs

    This cozy home
      I found love when alone

No one will take
this place from my heart

    This took years to build
I won't fall apart

Michael Tavon

## As

Just As the river knows
When to allow the wind
To guide its direction

I know when to go with the flow
I won't burden my soul
With things out of my control

Just as the clouds know
when to rain - it may pour for days

I know there will
be better days ahead
I can't dwell on the past
What's done won't change

As Father Time
blesses me with more hours to spend

I refuse to go broke
On shame and regret
I'll treasure the time spent
Til the day I meet my ends

As trees know when to shade
My passion for life will never fade,
And I'll be grateful, always

## Ocean Blue/Beautiful Life

I've come much too far
 to tread in muddy waters again

I see my path
When I swim in a clear ocean

I no longer fear drowning.
In my shallow past

Knee-deep and steady
I won't stumble on this path.

Crystal blue visions
Calm like gentle tides

Saltwater memories
Won't swell my eyes

I've found my paradise.
No grey clouds in my sky

I'm grateful
To have found this beautiful life

Michael Tavon

## Stevie Wonder Has More Life in His Eyes Than Most

Too many people live
with their eyes wide open
—- still blinded to the beauty
Around them choosing to dwell
In gloom without realizing
there's plenty of light ahead

It's abundantly clear,
Some have no desire
To see life as a precious gift
—- How rare it is to be alive

Despite the hardships,
never take your fresh air blessings
And moonlit manifestations
For granted

Within the blink of a second
It all could swiftly vanish
Like sand in the wind

Never forget to fill
Your latitude with gratitude
— Watch the life around you flourish

Life is a song
waiting to be written by you

## The Landlord II

There's a home inside your heart
waiting to be filled with peace
After you heal from
The grief that resides there
Find the courage to evict
When the lease is up

Michael Tavon

## <u>Soft Explosion</u>

You have a terrible habit of internalizing your pain. Once
you express the feelings you buried deep into the depths of
your heart, the boiling fire inside you erupts like a volcano.
Your fear of conflict caused this implosion. I hope you stop
letting your pain fester like an apple sliced open one day.
Speak your piece to keep your peace, even if that means
burning bridges you'll never cross again.

## **Frank Ocean Taught Me**

If I could go back in time
And rewrite my mistakes in pencil
I would laugh at the possibility
My mistakes aren't regrets
There's no need to
fix the errors of my life
to chase perfection
would be a waste of time
I prefer to keep writing

Typos gave my story
More character
And my poor choices
added richness to my arc
that makes my life more interesting

those flaws and mistakes
shaped me into who I am today
erasing anything I've done
would only create a false narrative
Despite every blip I've made
I became someone I'm proud of.

Michael Tavon

## While Listening to Mirrors by Justin Timberlake

I no longer see misery
When my reflection
Stares back at me

Staring back at me
Is the reflection
Of a clear smile, misery faded

Mirrors were time machines
I would travel to the past
Searching for moments
I couldn't get back

No need to go back
I've found peace in letting go
I only travel to where love is
My time machine captures the present

Happiness was a mirage
Fake smiles were worn like a suit
I didn't recognize my image
My reflection was dead

My reflection is alive
I adore the person I see
My smile - a suit of armor
Happiness ~ no longer a facade

## Sublime

My heart became lighter
once I released the burden
Of wanting to be understood
by everyone.

These days,
I allow my emotions
to flow in metaphors
I am poetry in motion

My aura is too sublime
For those who can't read
between the lines

Michael Tavon

*I hope you* fall in love with your reflection someday. I hope
when you see yourself, you see the masterpiece you've
been working on for so long. I hope you no longer
recognize the version of yourself who believed in giving
up. I hope you see a person who is worthy of grace. And
when your reflection stares back at you, I hope you smile
and say welcome home.

## **Anchor**

Steadfast & unbreakable
You have an anchor for a heart

When on the verge
of drowning
You cast love to
stay afloat

You've sailed amid violent waters
And always found your way to shore

You have an anchor for a heart
Steadfast & unbreakable

There is not a sea
You can't conquer

An entire world
Exists within you

Michael Tavon

## MUSEum

My mind is an art gallery
Of beautiful memories as photographs
And splattered thoughts on canvases

A mosaic of dreams
The colors coordinate so well

Statues made of stone
To immortalize my smile

Look what I've made
out of this life of mine

This marvelous life despite
The heartache and tears

Everything I love,
On full display right here

Take a walk through this gallery
when you're feeling down

You'll see clips of me swinging
With my feet to the sky as a child

Watch a movie about my youth
I hope it makes you laugh too

Then listen to songs about
my heartache and love

My mind is an art gallery
Come, explore
Hopefully, you'll leave
More inspired than
you were before

Michael Tavon

## **Portrait**

Your portrait of self-love
Will not be painted
In all pretty hues
Some colors will be dark
Some ~ ugly too
When the work is done
You will unveil
The most beautiful version
Of you

### 3 strikes

I'm a very forgiving person
But cross me three times
You won't find yourself back
on my good side

Don't take my kindness for weakness
Because I'm strong enough to know
When to let go

Michael Tavon

## Sound Watching

*Noon —- 3:38 pm*

A choir of blue jays
Sing with their chests
Outside my window
their song - louder than usual
We spring out of bed
The tune stops
They knew it was time
to stop dreaming
It's a beautiful day to live

The coffee maker brews
The sound of rain echoes
When it pours, mocha
Into my mug

Tires run against roads
60 miles per hour
I wonder where they're rushing to go,
Work? Starbucks? Mistress?
Who knows

*Night - 1:50 am*

As darkness dawns the sky
Spotted by stars amid the twilight

## To Build a Home

A gentle wind tickles the leaves
stray cats and raccoons
Search for food under the tree

Crickets play their lullaby
Like an orchestra
A soothing rhythm for the soul

Tires run against roads
40 miles per hour
I wonder why are they driving
So slow?
They are in no rush to get home

Michael Tavon

## <u>Type Love</u>

You deserve the kind of love that gives you the medicine
you need to heal from your old wounds. The type of love
that understands your pain. The kind of love that is patient
with past versions of you as you learn to navigate through
the phases of healing. The type of love that doesn't demand
perfection. You deserve a love --- pure and unconditional.

***I was so hard on myself***
I'm still healing from the bruises
A self-inflicted emptiness
I felt like a stranger in my skin
It took a long time for me
To fall in love with my reflection
It is a beautiful place to be
I will grow old here

Michael Tavon

## There's No Lemon So Sour

For all the sour days
 a bitter aftertaste will be left
Comes a chance to
Make the next day sweet

"There's no lemon, so sour
that you can't make
something resembling lemonade,"
A wise man once said.

So, squeeze every drop of sour
out of each miserable moment
to create something beautiful

Your grief will bloom into a blessing
Only after you redefine the meaning
Behind the suffering

## **Desperation**

I used to be so desperate for love
I fell for every mirage
I saw through my blurry eyes

Looking for love when love
wasn't looking for me
Led me to dead ends
Time and time again

After my last heartache
I vowed to love myself more
A long journey I had to travel
But it was worth every mile

Michael Tavon

## An Old Friend, Turned New

I'm so relieved to know you forgive me. Part of me needed
to hear those words, so the wound of losing you could
finally heal. Over the years, my silence created distance.
Not having you as my friend left a hole of 'what ifs' that
only got filled with doubt in my heart. Once acknowledged
my part in our fallout, you did the same and met me with
grace. As we begin to mend this broken bridge, this isn't a
do-over or a pick-up where we left off. It's an introduction
to who we've grown into since falling apart. Since this is a
second chance, I'm eager to meet my new friend.

## **Victim Blaming**

You've become
a master of deflection
When accountability is thrown
In your direction

Then question why
The same cycles repeat
The truth is bitter
But playing the victim is sweet

Your fingers are fatigued
From pointing blame
It's never your fault
You ignore the errors of your ways

You gotta open your eyes
 to see the big picture
Reflect on your mistakes
When you stare into the mirror

You can't keep deflecting
If you want to move on
Part of maturing is knowing
when to say you're wrong

Michael Tavon

## **Gratitude: Mantra**

I thank the universe
For blessing me with life
I thank my intuition for being my
Compass when I feel lost
I thank the universe
For blessing me with love
I thank the stars for being my
Compass when I feel lost

**<u>I Miss You: Duplex</u>**

When I close my eyes and reminisce
I'd be lying if I said I don't miss you

I miss you - life is a poem
written in stone, I can't change what's done

I wouldn't change a thing if I could
Doubt kills joy; I just want to be free

I want to be free. Do you forgive me?
I didn't push you away; I gave you space

I gave you space; you created
a whole universe without me

I see a whole universe without you
When I close my eyes and reminisce

Michael Tavon

## Non-Responsive

Choose your battles wisely
— You can't fight them all.

To protect your peace
You must know when to speak
And when not to respond

    Treat your tour time and energy
    Like precious gems
    By not wasting them
    On people who don't appreciate
    Your value

You'll only be draining yourself
When you try to fight every battle
That crosses your path

The art of self-control
Will take years of practice
To master — be patient

    When something triggers you
    Take a deep breath
    Step back - Before reacting

Don't allow those impulsive emotions
Get the best of you

## The Victim II

There's no winning
When you always
play the victim
If you wish to heal
It's time to get
That out your system

## **Dichotomy**

We don't think about
What we must lose
To gain what we want

How tragedies and miracles
Occur within the same breath
Of time

This life requires us
To weigh the good and bad
On the same scale
So balance won't get lost
Overtime.

Enjoy your wins,
But never get too lost
in the clouds
And lose who you are

Cry through the grief
But don't sulk too deep in misery
You'll find yourself
Digging from the bottom

The dichotomy of it all
Life can be so beautifully complex

## **The Train**

I hope my train ride to heaven
Is gorgeous
I hope I get the chance
To revisit the memories
I cherish before I depart

I hope death is just as beautiful
As the life, I've been blessed to live,
I don't want my exit to be bleak
Because being sad is easy

When my train leaves
I want to be free
— at peace

Instead of calling it the end
It will be the start
Of something wonderful

Michael Tavon

## **<u>The Collection</u>**

little memories become mementos
To keep near and dear to the heart

As time fades
Those beautiful memories
Become more difficult to let go

Life is a collection
of precious jewels
— a rare sight to behold
A worth no amount
Of money or time can measure

So as we stand
On earth, as it turns
Let's collect as many memories
As we can, and appreciate
Every step of the way

When it's time to let go
We'll leave this earth empty
With a trail of memories
For our loved ones to adore for eternity

## **The Birds: Prism**

Birds
Sing with joy
A pretty hymn of hope
When night becomes yesterday -
Sunshine promises more time for change

Birds
Sing when sad
To set their wings free
After being caged for a lifetime
Songs are like poems for the unheard

Birds
Are like me
Catching Melodies
When there's little to believe
Our voices carry us to new heights

Michael Tavon

## Art of Letting Go

I know my worth
So, if you wish to leave
I'll make it easy for you

I won't hold my breath
I've mastered the art of letting go

Why would I fight to shine
Into dark spaces that only
Overshadow my light

So leave if you want to
But I won't be here
If you come again

And I love myself too much
To beg you to stay

For you,
I'll make leaving me easy
But coming back will be Impossible

If you decide to go, don't expect me
To help you mend the bridge you've burned

## **Free Yourself**

Some say,
moving on is giving up
I believe,
moving on is self-love
When holding on
holds you back

   Why weaken your soul
   By squandering your strength
   To fight for what's already
   Dead and gone?

letting go of everything
that burdens you,
Will be the strongest act of courage
You will ever perform

   If you desire to
   heal into the best version of you,
   The real you

It's time to free yourself
Your future self will thank you

Michael Tavon

## I Would Never

I would never fill your mind
With clouds of doubt
After seeing how bright
The sun shines on your smile
When you express your dreams and wishes

I would never throw shade
Like a tree, but I will cool you down
When you can't stand the heat

I will be there to support
You in any way you need me
I will help your grass grow greener
Without turning into the color of envy
From beginning to end
Your dream is my dream

## Answer Me This

Why do you overthink
so often that
You fail to acknowledge
The ethereal power you possess.

Why do you
stack bricks of self-doubt
so high
Until you are unable
to see the beauty
On the other side
Of the walls you've built?

Why do you bite your tongue
to swallow your truth
Why would you rather
hurt yourself
Than tell people
How you truly feel?

why do you try to escape reality
When life doesn't go your way,
When will you realize,
No matter how far you run
Your problems will
Remain attached
Like a shadow

Michael Tavon

## **Dead Flames**

I don't believe in rekindling dead flames
that burned me every chance they received
so once I release the ashes of our past off into the wind,
there's no way we will recapture what we once had.

## <u>Maze</u>

I often lose myself in the maze of productivity by trying to
fill every waking moment with work. I become
overwhelmed trying to prove the voices in my head wrong -
to prove I am worthy of my blessings. I lose sleep chasing
my dreams. I must remind myself - rest is revolutionary
and sometimes, being still is more than enough.
I don't want to kill my peace by being overproductive.

Michael Tavon

***Find your balance,***
so you can remain centered
during turbulent times.

There will be **days** *the universe will test your patience* to see if you'll fold under pressure. It will come in waves of minor inconveniences or a stranger poking at your peace of mind. When that day arrives, don't fall for the traps. Take a step back and remember stress is temporary, so don't fall victim to creating a permanent consequence based on a fleeting emotion.

Michael Tavon

## **Chapters**

I'm still adding chapters to my story; I'm not ready to close
the book yet. There's so much life ahead, and I'm eager to
meet my future self. I'm ready for the peaks, valleys, clear
skies, and thunderstorms. I'm strong enough to handle it
all. I also know I'm not alone. ***My story isn't finished.*** My
pen is still alive, and the empty pages in my notepad are
waiting for my words to make a home out of them.
Whatever life throws at me I'll be ready to claim.

## Fine-tuning

After I repaired the brokenness
Inside me, I still have work to do

I constantly fine-tune
And tighten loose screws
To improve my state of mind

I discover new ways to breakthrough
When I breakdown,
Because nothing will stop me from
Pushing forward

When I become complacent
In my present space
I remember there's no growth
In the comfort zone

I refuse to settle for where I am
though I've traveled so far

There's so much road ahead
I can't leave a mile unspent

The work is never done
There's always room
For improvement

Michael Tavon

## **Shrinking**

If you find yourself
Shrinking down
To fit in with a crowd
you're surrounded by
The wrong people

You shouldn't have to
make yourself small
To be accepted
Into a circle

If they can't handle
All of you
They don't deserve
To experience half of you

So be big and loud
Shine without fear
You'll attract the people
Who are meant for you
When you stop trying to impress
The wrong people

## <u>Worth</u>

know your worth
If they have the audacity
To put you through hell and worst
have the strength
To put yourself first
*A faithful love*
*Is what you deserve*

Michael Tavon

## **Heartworking**

My heart is the hardest
working employee
I know,

No smoke breaks,
No Sick Days, no PTOs

It beats every moment
This precious life has to offer
Without a complaint

My heart
Enjoys working here
It tells me every day

I'm eternally grateful
To have been blessed with
Such a hard-working heart
I'll never lose sight of that

My heart never wants
a raise or promotion

But one day, it made
3 requests

To Build a Home

1. stop worrying
about the future
2. Stop doubting myself
3. Show more gratitude

Because it would
make its job a lot easier
If I didn't create problems
By stressing over
things I can't control

Michael Tavon

*(For Those Healing from a Breakup)*

The close of a chapter marks the possibility for a new story to begin. When the grief inside you grows faint, turn the page and return to loving yourself again. Your story deserves to be written with paragraphs of joy. Don't allow the bleak memories of a broken love to overshadow the blank pages waiting to be filled. Reclaim your voice, your story goes beyond heartache. People like you deserve to find happiness.

## **<u>Home</u>**

No strong house is built on an unstable foundation, so please take your time when building the best version of yourself. Don't rush the process; allow all the grief and pain to transform into the stones you'll use to build a new home.

Michael Tavon

## Break From Reality

Sometimes you need a break from reality. Trying to keep
up with everything happening in the world gets exhausting.
Escape the world to clear your mind without an ounce of
guilt in your heart. Don't be shackled like a prisoner by the
news or social media. You deserve to be free. You deserve
to be blissfully ignorant sometimes. If you're the type who
cares deeply about the things you feel, protect your peace
by not engaging with negativity. You deserve solitude from
time to time.

To Build a Home

"You must meet your healing halfway.
You must put in the work,
nothing comes easy."

Michael Tavon

**Sometimes it's Not
as Loud as We Think**

My depression was a Library,
Comfy and silent
~ tone-deaf
To the violent
devastation inside me,
Lost in my mind
No compass to guide me
Smiling while gently
Falling apart,
thoughts scattered Like stars

My depression,
played the greatest trick
Of them all

My shell painted
With vibrant shades
To show signs of life,
But the inside was a grave
I lived on the edge
To feel closer to death
A piss poor soul,
Fooling myself to be happy

## To Build a Home

When I needed help
Comfort was the zone,
I never felt alone

Depression made a home,
inside me

It was silent like meditation
Oblivious to the pain
I was escaping
Chasing the highs
To balance my lows
Coughing from clouded lungs
Til I felt numb

Depression was a drug

## The Dark That Comes to Light

What's left in the dark dies
Without a chance for revival

Your pain and regrets
Will Fester in the cold
Of darkness
If you keep hiding them there

Bring your truth into the open
There is beauty in transparency

The only way to grow
from your mistakes
Is to shed light
On the darkness inside of you

## **I'm Tired of Sad Black Poems**

I've written enough of them
The struggles, the plights
The anxiety that travels
down my spine
When I see flashing lights
In the rearview

No more sad black poems
No more lynchings and burnings
No more telling white folks
Which words they shouldn't say
When they speak to me
No more telling my own
I'm more than black enough
I'm fucking exhausted

I deserve
More happy black poems
I don't want to carry this burden
For a mile longer

My laughter is a song
hoods and suburbs
Can dance to

I've been sad and black
for far too long
this pen is tired
of singing my pain

No more sad black poems
I'm free and my smile

Michael Tavon

Symbolizes how beautiful black
Can be when black joy
Is brought to life

No more sad black poems from me
I'll change the world
 with my love today

## A Man's Pride

The pride of a man
Is too heavy
To talk about heartache

We cry in silence
Where we are only
heard by our shadow

We grieve through
Liquid bottles and strip clubs
— Poems are too soft
& therapy is a lonely place

A man's ego can't afford
to be vulnerable again
So we go broke through vices -
Devices we use to cope

Losing balance
On the slackline of hope -
Heartbreak is a sudden
Descent from grace

We're afraid to face
How we feel
We don't want to appear weak
So we hurt others
Before we heal ourselves

Dear men,

Michael Tavon

There's nothing weak
About seeking help
You need to open
Your heart to heal
The burdens you carry

## **Legacy**

The day my ascension arrives
I hope they remember me
By the love I exude when I smile
And the tenderness in my voice

I hope my legacy
Leaves an infectious energy
I don't want to fade
The way some memories do

I fear and loathe
The thought of being forgotten

Before I die
I will leave my mark behind

Love is what they'll remember me by

Michael Tavon

## People like You

People like you are stronger than given credit for. You
bend over backwards for people who step over you, but
spreading joy still comes more naturally than breathing.
The world uses your kindness as a crutch to support their
dead weight, but you don't let them break you. Despite
being everyone's favorite afterthought, you never hesitate
to save a loved one from their misery. You find reasons to
smile with a heart permanently scarred and bruised. People
like you have infinite reasons to become heartless, but
you're stronger than the environment around you. Love
conquers all, and you've defeated all odds. You're stronger
than what you're given credit for. Never forget that.

## **Time Travel**

Stop looking into the future; it doesn't exist. Today, this present moment is the only blessing guaranteed. Soak in love. Open your eyes to the light. The more you reach for the future that seems too elusive to grab, the more misery you'll bring to your beautiful heart. Appreciate every step you take. The present is a present, cherish it, or you will look back on your journey with miles of regret for overlooking everything you had in front of you.

Michael Tavon

## Alien

Nothing feels lonelier than being
an outsider in your own home,

You spend so much time
with your head in the clouds
The ground seems too shaky to step on

You dream in color
'Cause reality is grey and white
So, you reside inside the paradise
You designed in your mind

Cause nothing feels lonelier than being
an outsider in your own home,

You wear your heart on a sleeve
Despite the world being cold
Your youth was tainted,
Somehow you remained gold

Ugly thoughts often
Travel through your beautiful mind
Lost between dark and light
Someday you'll realize
Heaven ain't hard to find
Even when nothing feels lonelier
than being alone in your own home

## **Compassion**

You must fight to survive
Constantly at war against
People who look like you,
People who don't like you,
And even your own mind

You constantly exhaust your energy
Combating and scratching against
The opposition
To protect everything you love
And stand for

Living our truth is a battle
Most of us will die fighting
Because half of humankind
lacks compassion

Michael Tavon

## To Those Who Need It

Your vibrant spirit
Does not need to fade too soon
You have a story of pain
Millions of people deserve to hear
Don't take that away from them
Your heart is humble
Your ears are always open
When you speak
I often close my eyes
So I can listen clearly
Your words are powerful,
The way you're willing
To give without a second
Thought is rare.
Please don't leave too soon
The world needs more of you

Your pain, your rage
The voices in your head
You must continue to battle
Don't let them win.
people need you
You're special to me, too.

## **<u>Old Me. Dead</u>**

The old me
  is so far gone
  We rarely got along
  When I tried to escape
  He tied me down, but I got away.

My old toxic friend
My beautiful enemy
His spiteful stares and
Lighthearted envy.

I was fooled once before
I don't need him anymore
Goodbye to the old me
My former friend
A relationship that needed to end

## **Searching for Myself**

Let me discover myself
Without judging my path
I will make mistakes,
I will burn and crash
The flames won't last
 I will learn from the past,
 Rise above the rubble and ash,

My life is not for you to understand
I'm afraid – I am brave
But this space, I won't stay
—

I will move on to grow

Side eyed stares
Stones you may cast
I'm not built like you
My heart is not glass

You won't break me,
Project your fears, I don't need you here
Be like magic, disappear

I'm searching for myself -
I will get lost along the way
The old me is gone
I will not beg you to stay
I am strong enough
To roam alone within my soul,
I will find a new home

## Healing is Uncomfortable

A thousand yesterday's held captive inside the brick walls in your mind, too stubborn to let go, you've found comfort in grief. Your future would have only been a mile away if you had stopped running in retrograde. You cry to the sky for the clouds to pour drops of solace while you're the one holding yourself back. You live in hell's comfort inn because moving on seems frightening to you.

When will you understand ~ healing will not meet you in your comfort zone. Growth only happens when you're ready to find a new home outside of the miserable yesterdays that reside in your mind.

Michael Tavon

**Exploration.**

The universe inside you is ready to be explored, so dream
infinitely. Your imagination is a superpower; your
sensitivity is a gift. With those, you intuitively possess the
ability to manifest the life you desire but don't get so high
in the clouds that you lose the ground of reality.
Remember, the journey is a marathon, so pace yourself.
Balance is key to unlocking your magic.

## Comfort Zone Penitentiary

Your mind is a haven, but you treat it like a prison by caging your potential behind metal bars for committing the crime of not pursuing your dreams. You've allowed doubt to shackle your hands and feet because not trying feels safer than failing. You've imprisoned yourself within your comfort zone, where you will slowly die disappointed and alone if you never cultivate the strength to find a new home.

Michael Tavon

## **Hometown**

As much as I miss you
It's impossible to ignore
The looming sadness
Beating in my heart
 Every time I come back

I often feel guilty
For discovering peace
In a different place

But every time I see you
I'm reminded why
It was best for me
To build a new home elsewhere

## **<u>Money Problems II</u>**

Even though.
we're in a better place
These days
My greatest fear is still
losing you
I fought so hard to have
you in my hands
I refuse to feel broke(n) again,

I shouldn't depend on you as much as I do
But I know what life is like without you
And I refuse to go back

You provide security
And everything I need
Honestly, you spoil me

They say the c.r.e.a.m doesn't buy happiness,
but I've never been happier since we met

I know — such a heavy burden
To place on your shoulders

As I grow older, I could only hope
This toxic obsession wanes over time

Michael Tavon

## **Money Problems III**

I lost years of sleep
fantasizing about what I would do
once I found you

I counted the ways
I'd hold you in my hands
And spend time with you

I lost so much of myself
Working overtime -
Hoping you'll meet me halfway

In lieu of loving myself
I became obsessed with the idea
Of you loving me

I lost pieces of my sanity
Chasing after something so fleeting

One day I'll realize
I can't depend on you
to make me happy
I must find that on my own

## <u>Another Poem About Money</u>

For so long, my mental health fluctuated like my bank
account. When I was broke, I was low; my mental state is
high when my money is right. It wasn't until recently I
realized how unhealthy my emotional attachment to money
is. I'm afraid of losing it; I often second-guess myself
before spending it on the things I dreamed of experiencing
when my pockets were low. Since balance is key, I gotta
learn how to balance my mental health and bank account
before they both break.

Michael Tavon

## **Happiness**

It may come and go
Like distant kin
Be sure to
Treasure the time spent
Because you'll never know
the next time you'll feel it again.

## Gentle Waters

You can be unstable as the waters your tread. There's no shame in the emotional depth you carry; you just need a life preserver to prevent drowning. Some days it's hard to navigate through the waves of your moods all alone, so don't push away the people you love when they offer and helping hand. It's okay to receive help. You can't be the one doing all the saving.

Michael Tavon

## <u>For You</u>

Don't allow fear
to hold you hostage
in your comfort zone
Believe you're enough
to step into the unknown.

## **People Like You III**

With all the obstacles thrown at you
You still wear a smile worth a million dollars

Even after all the times
People tried to break you
You never shattered like glass
You remain soft like a feather,
But still, as tough as they come

People like you don't give up
When waves don't flow in your direction
You swim against the currents
To get to your destination

I'm happy you're still here
to share your story
People like you deserve
To be heard

Michael Tavon

## Like Thor's Lil Bro

A lowkey life is peaceful
I learned this
once my circle got smaller
And started going out less

As I matured
The fear of missing out
became faint, I was at ease with
Not being in the mix

With fewer people in my orbit
I have more time to spend
With myself

Being lowkey gives
Me the space to be free
When I got older
I cared less about popularity

## Streams

I enjoy watching others find their happiness. Like how joy exudes from their smile when they talk about the things they love. Or the way the ground lights up when they're following the journey meant for them. Or when their body speaks a language of confidence because they've learned to love every inch of their being. There's something beautiful about witnessing someone coming into their own unapologetically. Even when the sky feels like it's falling behind me, watching others be happy gives me something to look forward to. We all carry pain like a bag of bricks; that's why it's inspiring to watch others grow into their happiness too.

Michael Tavon

**Film: duplex**

If a picture is worth a million words
Film all the smiles you can

    A smile on film is a piece of joy immortalized
    collect them before there is none left to capture

This ride won't last forever
capture all the beautiful moments along the way

    So many beautiful moments are worth remembering
    for a lifetime, film them all so you won't forget

Before you forget - Film all the smiles
memories fade, but pictures last forever

    But forever doesn't exist
    Enjoy the good times you're blessed to get

Good times are priceless
And a picture is worth a million words

## **Silver lining:  Duplex**

I dream of silver linings
 On rainy days

    Rainy days are beautiful when
    they don't drown me. I pray for clear skies

Prayers and mantras
Manifest into brighter tomorrow's

    Tomorrow gives birth to a new perspective
    When the storm passes

I no longer fear storms
 when they come

    When storms come
    I see beauty behind the chaos

I know how beautiful chaos can be
Like a silver lining on rainy days

Michael Tavon

## Yes, I Fear Dementia

I fear dementia more than any disease
I don't wanna live inside a hollow mind

Give me cancer, something
I'll have the chance to beat

Give me a noble death
Like saving a family
From their burning home

I fear dementia more than any disease
I don't want my brain to dry up and rot
Like crops with no water

I want to be present until my final breath
God, please don't give me the saddest death

Give me a death I can remember
If that makes sense at all

I want to be able to tell
My family and friends
How much I love them before I go

Please, God whatever you do
Don't curse me with dementia

## The Saddest Disease

The one when the victim's brain
Becomes a daisy
As time plucks their memories
Until there's nothing left to remember

The one when you
Repeat their name like a mantra
But they never answer your prayers
Of coming back to who they used to be

They become lost inside themselves
A fate they don't understand -drifting away
They can't be saved

Losing their mind, bowels, and balance
No control over what's next
This cruel disease has no peace

A slow death sentence
For the imprisoned
Relatives can't recognize
Who they see when they visit

Just a messy corpse
That holds breath but no memory

Michael Tavon

## **30 going on 50?**

I notice new grays sprouting
From my scalp every morning now
I water some like flowers
I pluck some like weeds

I'm thankful for this garden of wisdom
Atop my head, but I pray
they don't spread too fast
 - I want to stay young for a while.

Many men my age begin
To shed every stupid thing
they've done strand by strand
As the edge of their fade recedes
Like a shoreline
My hair is full
Of reminders of all the
Good, I've done

Turning gray isn't half bad
Because I am proud of everything
I had to overcome
For this beautiful garden to grow

## Alone With My Shadow

Self-doubt is my shadow
Trailing every step as I progress
Through darkness
When I moved forward from the past
I look back to see him
Looming over my shoulder
To remind me I'm not alone,
He mocks my every attempt
To evade,
I tell myself I'm doing great
I say in due time
I'll see the light,
I won't go out without a fight
I throw punches with all my might
Hoping one will strike him down
He hurries and disappears for a while,
Long enough to convince
My mind, I'm finally free,
The joy is short-lived
When I see his image
Dark, wide, silent, but loud
Staring from behind
I sulk at the thought
Of someday
Sharing the same coffin as him

Michael Tavon

## (A Layer of Self-Love is *Understanding* Your Inner Child)

Your inner child is far from home
Searching for a new place to stay
After being neglected for too long

Why do you keep pushing
Your inner child away
Treating the softest part of you
Like an afterthought

Your inner child deserves
To be held and told how magic
They are -

Your inner child sees
the stress in your eyes
And wants you to smile again.

How do you expect to heal
If you refuse to listen
To the child crying inside you?

Understanding is a layer of self-love
Don't let your pride
Be the reason why
You lose your inner child

## A Message from Your Inner Child

Please don't leave me behind
I wanna travel with you
I hate being alone

Please don't let heartache turn you
into someone, I don't know
I'm still afraid of monsters,

Can I have a cookie or two,
I promise to be good

Why do you cry so much?
Did I do something wrong
I promise not to do it again

Take me outside when the sun is out
I'm also afraid of the dark

If no one hasn't said it in a while
I'm proud of you

You make me happy
When you smile
You should do it more often

Michael Tavon

## **A Message From Your Inner child II**

I forgive you for neglecting me
It wasn't your fault,
You were lost and couldn't find
Your north star

When you grew up, we grew apart
And that hurts me the most
I thought we would always be close
Like two peas in a pod

I yearned to be close to you
When I needed warmth, you turned cold
Please come back to me
I will welcome you with open arms

No grudges will be held
We can pick up where we left,
So much has happened
Since the last time we met
I'll tell you all about it
When I see you again

## Say Hello To

I would never abandon my inner child
Because they didn't give up on me
During my darkest hour

Young heart, old soul
Vibrant and hopeful

When my mind didn't
My inner child always
knew where to go

I vow to never be a deadbeat
To the purest part of me

My heart is free
Because my inner child
Still lives within me

Michael Tavon

**A Home**

## **Songs We Love Together: Duplex**

For the songs, we love to vibe to
A playlist that symbolizes our union

To symbolize our bond, we send songs
as love notes to make each other smile

I smile when lyrics remind me of you
A gentle hug for the soul

  Hug me close when you send
  Sweet melodies for my ears to hear

My ears love to hear
What your heart wants to say

  Don't keep a single thought a secret
  Our love grows stronger through music

watering our hearts with music, we grow stronger
through the songs, we love to vibe to

Michael Tavon

## Color Me Crazy

When my mood turns bluer
Than Chicago's night skyline
And all red hell burns behind
My white smile
Will you gaze into my brown eyes,
And say everything will be fine?

When thoughts darker than
The deepest depths
 of the Arctic Ocean
Rush to the surface
Of my grey-pink mind
Will you embrace my brown skin
 with heavenly openness
To help me feel less hopeless?

It's not your job to save me,
But when sorrow comes to use
My body as a canvas
Will you color me crazy
Or paint some soft bright hues
On my dark, weary heart?

I need to know,
before I let my walls down,
 for you

## **How to Love Him**

When a man spills his deepest feelings
Don't make a bigger mess by
Making his pain about you

Be his sanctuary
— A place where
his soft side isn't met with shame

As men, we loath peeling back our layers
Because we fear our partner
will invalidate how we feel

His heart isn't made of stone
So don't treat him like he's dead inside

When he puts his heart on a sleeve
Make him feel warm
Don't turn a cold shoulder
When the truth bruises your ego

He deserves compassion too
Listen when he's hurting
If you don't want to lose him

Michael Tavon

## Chef's Kiss

She takes pride in feeding me
The stove becomes a canvas
When cooking up a masterpiece

Every dish she prepares
Is seasoned with care
Her soul food - the answer to my prayers

I'm never disappointed
When the food hits my tongue
I crave more when my plate is done

From baked goods to pasta
Every dish is a work of art
She knows good food is the key to my heart

## I Love Me Some You

I adore the way your smile,
Spreads like bad news
When I hug you from behind

I love me some you
My hands can't get enough
A sweet addiction you've become

I adore the way you do chores
In those shorts I like,
You keep the house clean
While I keep a dirty mind

I love me some you
I don't mind staying home
Moments are never dull
You make the rainy days fun

I adore every breath you take,
The morning ones too
Color me crazy but I love me, some you

Michael Tavon

## Why I Fell in Love W/U

If your mind has ever wondered why
I fell in love with you; the answer is

You didn't need to be saved
It was refreshing to find
Someone I didn't have to put on a cape for

I didn't have to leap hurdles
To get past any trust issues
Or climb walls to get to the real you

Of course, you weren't perfect
Or completely healed from heartaches
No one is,
But your baggage
Was lighter than most

You never tried to revive dead connections
Which gave us the space
To innerstand each other without
The pressure of competing with ghosts

You made falling in love a gentle descent

## <u>Still</u>

I've explored every part of you
ten thousand times,
And your love still feels new

The butterflies in my stomach
Still rise when you say goodnight

After all this time
My heart still has a crush on you

Michael Tavon

When I close my eyes
And think of the moment
My life changed forever
The first thing I see – *you*

## My Light

You don't depend on the wind
to guide your direction
You're the aura of earth
that has my soul connected
On another level,
intertwined with your heart
I can feel what you feel
even when apart

Michael Tavon

My life became
Far less complicated
The moment you
Professed your love for me
That's when I knew
I found my soulmate

## Weight

They say love puts weight on you

Well, Extra love fills my gut and waist
I can no longer slip into
 my favorite pants from high school
my tees hug my skin tighter

When people say I look happy
That means they notice,
how much I filled my once slight frame

They say love puts weight on you
I've gained twenty-one pounds of love
Because of her

She feeds me good,
She loves me right

I rest with a full heart every night

Michael Tavon

## **Home at First Sight**

I fell in love with you
Because you felt like home
At first sight

I fell in love with you
Because life became so much easier
The moment when you arrived

I fell in love with you
Because you know your worth
And would not accept a dollar less

I fell in love with you
Because you are my bright spot
in this dark mess

See, I fell in love with you
Because your essence
Has an ethereal glow

I fell in love with you
Because you didn't need me

When a relationship is healthy
It creates the space for love to grow

## **<u>Carefree Girl</u>**

I love watching you move carefree
As you sway your hips so casually
Vibing to the beat of the song
Like you're in a world of your own

So pure, so secure

In your skin, so confident
The mirror is your friend,
In your panties and bra
Stretch marks resembling shooting stars,

I yearn to touch those craters too
Every part of you,
Sends me to the moon

Michael Tavon

## **Ladybug**

The love you give is like a ladybug
landing on my skin ~ gentle & rare

And I keep you safe upon descent
My deepest fear is watching you slip away

I handle with care
As you explore my layers
Your love ~ a gentle hug from heaven

My blood flows like a river,
Under a calm breeze
When you touch me

They say,
when a ladybug lands on you
Good fortune will ensue

Since the day you said, "I love you."
I've been the luckiest person
On this side of the sun

## Thunder & Sunshine

Love is not a storm. Love should never cause thunder to rumble in your heart. Some days will be dark and grey clouds will loom, but your partner shouldn't be the reason why it rains.

Love is supposed to make you feel safe amid the storms life brings. You shouldn't have to fight for sunny days. You shouldn't have to cry for clear skies.

If you feel like you're in an endless cycle of chaos and disrespect, what you have is not love, my friend; it's a hurricane -- evacuate before it kills you.

Michael Tavon

## You're My Sky

One of my greatest joys
Since the day our worlds
Became one
is watching you illuminate
My life like sunrise
I'm marveled by your presence every day

See, my love, you fill the sky
with so much color
It's been a pleasure
To see you leave the darkness behind
And become the light you are

You took the storms life handed you
and created rainbows

I'm a heart-shaped cloud in this life of yours
And you've graced me
With the chance to watch you glow

As each moment
Fades into a new yesterday
I will never forget the person
I fell in love with

As I eagerly await to meet the sunrise
You'll become tomorrow —

— Who you are today
Is all the sunshine I need

To Build a Home


Loving you is a season
Of gorgeous weather
And I will be here to gaze
 for a lifetime

Michael Tavon

## **Tranquil**

Rest your head
On my heart, so you can hear
The sound of tranquility
When you sleep

## Vinyl Love

There's a rhythm my heart moves to
And a harmony my thoughts carry
since the day I met you
Your love is a record
That I will spin,
Until the needle breaks

Michael Tavon

## **Sunflower Field**

My heart made peace
With all the love lost
Before finding you
Which created the space
For our bond to bloom
Like a sunflower field

## <u>Dreams</u>

When I close my eyes, it's you
Flying through the clouds under a sky blue
When I dream, all I see is you
When I close my eyes, it's you

Michael Tavon

## Lover's Pledge

If I ever betray your heart
I hope you have the strength
To leave me where I stand

Believe when I say I know better,
If I give anything less,
Please take the ring off your hand

Promise me,
No amount of apologies
Or grand gestures
Will convince you to take me back

This is my pledge
Right hand on my chest
I'll do everything to make sure
We don't become a love of the past

I won't give you a reason to leave
Your love is a tattoo
Forever embedded in my heart

You're all I need for every year to come
You have a special hold on me
And I'll never let us drift apart

## **<u>Goodnight, Love II</u>**

As the world goes dark,
You and I share kisses
like candy to see whose
Lips are sweeter —

I can feel your smile
With my eyes closed —
It brings me joy to know
You rest with a happy heart
each passing moon

I love you, I love us
This life — all I ever wanted

I've dreamed of this love
for countless hours,
When my bed was half empty.

Please pinch me,
When the sun says good morning
Waking up next to you
Feels so surreal

Michael Tavon

## **Special Love**

You love me in a way
That makes my spirit smile

The type of love that gives my soul
a heaven on earth

The type of love
I can't see myself living without

The type of love where trust is home
And my heart feels safe with you

I could never thank you
Enough for loving me
The way you do

## <u>Talk it Out</u>

We've come too far to let
a disagreement break us apart
Let's sit down, talk it out
Hear each other out

Your point of view
is as valid as mine,
let's take the time
To understand each other's mind

There's no need to yell,
Fight, or cry.
We're mature enough to find a solution
Without causing pain

Michael Tavon

## **At ODDs**

Rough patches can be sewn
When communication is right
So instead of letting this tear us apart
Let's use this opportunity
To mend a deeper understanding
So our bond grows
Stronger than ever before

## **True Happiness**

I'm happy your entire world doesn't revolve around me.
You don't suffocate me with codependency; your love -- a
breath of fresh air. You have a life outside of me, so there's
no pressure to cater to any form of loneliness. We are both
whole beings - individually, which makes our relationship
complete.

Michael Tavon

## Beautiful Addiction

Since the hands of yours
and mine first intertwined
Not A moment has gone by
That I don't feel loved
As the hands of time
slow dance around the clock
Each moment between you and I
Is filled with the type of love
Only the stars and moon
can relate to
Baby, you're the sun to my sky,
we bring each other light
so warm and bright
when the world becomes a storm,
We find solace in the rain
Our love is a home
I can't get enough of you
You're my beautiful addiction

## <u>Sobbing on Tuesdays</u>

The nights we crawl
into each other's arms and sob,
While watching *This Is Us,*
is one of the many reasons I cherish
Our bond

A sacred ritual between you and I
Tissues on Tuesdays
There's no shame when we cry

Our hearts and these stories - intertwined
We see pieces of ourselves in each storyline

And when we can't relate
We take the chance
to gain a new perspective

When the episode ends
We take a deep breath
And reflect as a collective

The Pearson's - near and dear
To our hearts and beyond
Oh, how we're going to miss
This show when it's gone

Michael Tavon

## **White Flag**

True love will never bring
out the worst in you
So, when you find yourself ,
Screaming to be heard,
Crying to be felt,
Or putting up walls
To push them away

it's time to wave the white flag
And call truce

Love should never feel like a war
So, if you feel like pieces of you are dying
While trying to keep the relationship alive

It's a sign, it's time to let go

 what's meant for you
should never be a struggle to keep

## <u>Angel</u>

It was a dream when I met you
My omnipresent angel
With crystal eyes
Shining bright whenever
you came through
Nothing less than beautiful
Your presence is a present
And the present is so fruitful

Michael Tavon

*Not a day too late*
*Nor a year too early*
*You and I crossed paths*
*At the perfect time*

***I'll be your peace***
When the world is at war
I'll be your shelter
When life becomes a storm

You'll never fear dying alone
No matter what comes
I'll be your home.

Michael Tavon

You and I
***Shall never drift apart***
Pieces of you will
forever float in my heart

To Build a Home

**For You**

Michael Tavon

### *The Apology You Owe to Yourself*

I apologize for pushing you away
When you needed a tight hug to reassure your worth.
  If I haven't said it before, *I love you wholeheartedly.*

Sorry, for the times
I was too hard on you for feeling lost
You deserve to know,
  ***You are my North Star***

I made you feel worthless
When self-doubt consumed me
  ***From here on, I vow to show mercy***

I'm sorry for ignoring your cries for help
All the mistakes I've made
  ***I'm still learning how to forgive myself***

I promise to be patient
I promise to be kind
I hope you forgive me
  ***I hope soon you'll be fine***

## The Apology You Owe To Yourself II

I'm sorry for losing my inner child
While chasing a life I wasn't meant to find

You deserved more balance
When my mind was a slackline

I'm sorry for pushing you away
When I thought you were leaving me behind

My pride refused to let me cry

I'm sorry for not listening
to my intuition when it told me where to go

I've always been hardheaded,
I had to learn on my own

I apologize for not loving you more
When you felt alone

I hope you know,
you've always been home

Please forgive me
For all the shit I put you through

Michael Tavon

*Note To Self:*

You feel worthless because the people
You go hard for desert you
But I love you, I hope that's enough

## A Message from Your Past Self

I know you're still healing
from the wounds I inflicted
-- every scar you see
Reminds you of my poor decisions

Could you find it in your
 heart to forgive me?

I was unstable like a ship with no anchor
I caused wreckage with my misguided anger

 I'm sorry for leaving you
 with my mess to clean

I tried the best I could
But I failed you a thousand times
I didn't protect you I'm the reason you cry

 Don't give up on me,
 I still deserve a warm hug

My foolish ways were a cry for help
While the world was tone deaf
I felt most alone
When I didn't love myself

 Please don't hold grudges,
 I just want my best friend back

Michael Tavon

Sometimes, a compromise is necessary
to improve the quality of a relationship,
but never compromise so much
to the point you become a shell of yourself

## **A Woman Called Home: Duplex**

No one is God on earth
There's only one way to enter this world

We enter this world through
a woman and call it home

Man enters a woman's warmth
and call her home

When men leave home, they leave it
rundown and empty like the women they love

Just like the women they love
They call earth home and ruin it the same

They ruin home and call it love; earth is a woman
one way to arrive - a thousand ways to leave

Men raise hell, then leave home
After policing wombs like they're Gods on Earth

Michael Tavon

***I would never***
Spray poison on someone's garden
Because my dreams have yet to
 bloom for harvest
I'm too focused on my progress
there's no need to envy
anyone's success

***When plans fail***,
and setbacks
slows down progress
Remember, rejection
Can lead to better opportunities

Michael Tavon

**Dirty**

Don't judge the dirt on my hands
When your sink is stained with mud
Give me a chance to learn from my mistakes
Before deeming me unworthy of grace

## A Message from Your Past Self II

As much as I love you
It's time to move on
I can't keep being
your scapegoat when
something goes wrong

(I *hope you know,*
*You're stronger than given credit for*)

You can't keep me hostage
For the rest of your years
You must let me go
But my love will always be near

Stop holding onto me,
I am not holding you back
If you truly care for me
You'd stop living in the past

Michael Tavon

## A Message from Your Past Self III

When I hear you speak
Such ugly things upon yourself
My inner child cries

*I wish you could see yourself*
*Through my eyes*

Since you refuse to say these words
I'll do it for you:

I'm proud of who you're blooming into,
I'm proud of what you had to overcome
To get to where you are today
You are everything I never was
More than anything I could have imagined

*The next time you decide to swim*
*In self-pity, think of me*

So you can see how much
you've grown since
The last time we kicked it

To Build a Home

*Focus on building*
*a home within yourself*
*before finding one with someone else*

Michael Tavon

## Maze of Thoughts

Get out of your fucking head
Most days, you get lost in a maze
Of thoughts as you try to figure out
the next move

you remain still like time is a statue
but no hour is going to wait for you
so what are you waiting for?
For the right moment?
When your stars align?

Stop overthinking
Put one foot ahead of the other
Growth does not show up
For those who are too afraid
To get out of their own way

To Build a Home

Loneliness can manipulate
Your heart into believing
A gentle connection is love
When it's only meant to be platonic.
Chasing a fantasy can lead to another
Heartache if you don't exercise caution

Michael Tavon

## **Brittle Wood**

A relationship built on loneliness
Is a house built with brittle wood
It may look pretty on the outside
But won't withstand stormy weather

Before falling in love again
Work on healing the wounds
From your past relationships

Don't fall into the cycle of moving home to home
Because you fear being alone

## <u>Sail On</u>

Once the ship sails
I will be gone
To the point of no return
You'll have to travel an ocean
To prove you're worthy
To sail with me again

Michael Tavon

*I would never* throw salt on someone's
healing wounds, my heart is too big to cause pain
when compassion is needed.

## **Build: Prism**

Stuck
In the past
Fleeting dreams turn faint
Where do you want to exist
The present is here; seize the day

Grow
From the pain
Sorrow is a drug
Don't get addicted to grief
When lost, find your way back to yourself

Meet
Love halfway
Where hope still resides
A space of transparency
Free yourself of the burdens your drag

Michael Tavon

## **Fuck Em**

Mean spirited people
Will spit on your dreams
And call it constructive criticism

You'll find yourself
Feeling alone when trying to build
An empire with fake friends

If their words make you feel small
Don't hesitate to cut them off

Your future can't be built
Off the strength of unstable support

To Build a Home

One day
You will find someone
Who won't feel pressured to love you
Because it will be second nature to them

Michael Tavon

You're damaged from the pain
Life put you through
Despite all of it
You give a divine energy
Through a heart that aches
*People like you are rare*

## **Processing**

Your mind deserves a rest
Put the phone away
You have no idea the stress
Your brain goes through
When processing content
That triggers negative emotions
Every second you scroll
Today is the perfect day
To live without social media

Michael Tavon

## **Gold: Prism**

Don't
Let anyone
Define who *you* are
Your story is gold plated
No one holds the power to break you

Break
Free from them
If they drain your soul
Leeches disguised as friends will kill
If they stick around for too long, move on


Don't
Let anyone
Call your home a wreck
It took a lot of pain to heal
Brick by brick, a pretty life you've built

To Build a Home

The world is so ill there's no cure
To heal this depression
The best we can do
Is ***take the little pockets of joy***
life allows us to hold
And treasure them like gems

155

Michael Tavon

### *Feels like we're all drowning*

Most of the world is so sad
I believe the oceans we swim
Are filled will tears
It's so easy to drown in that feeling
It takes years of swimming
To find peace
A great deal of strength
is required to choose joy

The world can be a cruel place,
Hope is a drought
and I pray you find your river
 before dying of thirst

You deserve an ever-growing love
Life is hard; no one should do this alone

***Defend your dreams***
Like an army
Don't let anyone
Steal your passion from you

Michael Tavon

***Dreamers are often misunderstood***
Because their reality is too bright
For those who see life as black and white

To Build a Home

*I **would never*** chase anyone to prove my worth
Time is my most precious commodity,
I won't spare a second running after someone
Who wants to leave.

Michael Tavon

*I would never* take gossip as gospel
Words heard through the grapevine
become wine-stained lies
over the rush of time
the truth gets lost in translation

my spirit is too rich
to listen to cheap gossip
keep loose lips tight around me
I don't care about negativity

To Build a Home

It's better to take baby steps
on the *path of healing*,
than to remain idle out of fear

Michael Tavon

## **Friends**

Some friendships aren't built to last
Others become monuments
Through the test of time

Sometimes it's hard to know
Which friends will you need to let go
And which friendships you
Should work on to keep close

History and milestones
Can cloud your judgment
But trust your intuition
It will never steer you wrong

***Apologizing to the person you've hurt*** reveals a great deal of growth within you. It shows you possess the strength to let go of your ego and admit you're wrong. It shows how well you navigate between pride and compassion. And after you express sorrow for how you treated them, you will feel much lighter because the weight of guilt will finally be lifted.

Michael Tavon

Any connection that leaves you empty
Is a connection not worth saving
Realize the damage it's causing
Before it kills you

## Future Self

Somewhere down the line
A healed version of you is thanking you,

Thanking you for working on yourself
Even when you didn't feel like clocking in

Thanking you for remaining patient
Because time is a doctor that heals all wounds

This version of you –
Learned how to love every broken part
Yes, even the parts you've deemed unworthy

Your future self is thanking you
for not giving up
When nothing went your way

You have a strong sense of belief
And nothing is heavy enough to break you

So, when thoughts of doubt storm your mind.

Remember, your future self
is somewhere thanking you
for becoming softer on yourself

Michael Tavon

You'll prolong your blessings by
Giving the wrong people second chances.

**Forgiveness** is a step towards healing,
but you don't have to keep holding on
to the people who are holding you back.

Keep this in mind,
removing **dead roots** clears space
for something more fruitful to grow.

## **Decluttering**

Protect your peace
By not cluttering your space
With people:

    1)   Who dangle broken versions
          Of yourself over your head,
          When you're on the path
          Of liberating yourself.

    2)   Use your past for ransom
          When they something from you.

    3)   Make you feel empty
          After spending time
          And above all.

    4)   Cross your boundaries
          Like a finish line
          Because they see
          Your compassion as a weakness
          They know you'll always
          Let them run back to you.

Your energy is too sacred,
Allowing these toxic people
In your home
Is the opposite of self-care.

Michael Tavon

*Happiness hits different* when you focus on watering the grass you were given without competing with your neighbors to see whose lawn is greener. Beauty takes time; growth can't be rushed. Take pride in what you have and put in the work to see it flourish. Other grass may be greener, but what you have is a blessing you were given.

To Build a Home

*When loving someone forces you to lose*
*Parts of yourself*, let them go before you find yourself
buried alive in a plot of confusion and disappointment.
Love isn't a grave; pieces of you shouldn't have to die to
make it work.

Michael Tavon

Be so devoted to your growth
The fakes will weed themselves
Out of your life for you.

The universe always has a way of
Working things out in your favor,
When you focus on loving yourself

To Build a Home

You pray to God for miracles
Without realizing you are one

Michael Tavon

*(After a breakup, take a break and focus on yourself)*

A breakup isn't a contest to see who can get over their
heartache faster. Don't race into the next relationship;
you'll lose that too. Don't over-stress your heart by
working overtime to avoid your emotions. Don't get lost on
the party scene to fake a facade of happiness. Recovery
requires patience. There are no shortcuts to healing a
broken heart. You gotta feel to heal, converse with your
heart; so you begin the process of moving on.

To Build a Home

## <u>HeartTalks</u>

Host conversations with your heart
To make peace with the broken
Parts of you that may never get fixed
Realize all versions of you deserve
A warm tight hug

Talk to your heart
Learn how to love where it hurts,
***Bold scars turn faint*** when nurtured

Michael Tavon

## **Phases**

You are like the moon,
all the phases you go through
You are worthy of grace

You have the right
shift, evolve, and change
When light eclipses
The darker sides of you
***Never let anyone pressure***
***Into remaining the same***

If people can marvel at
The ever-changing moon

They can do the same for you
When you evolve into a brighter you

## **Healing Wounds**

You deserve the kind of love that gives you the space to
heal from your old wounds. The type of love that
understands your pain and the life you had before them.
The type of love that doesn't demand perfection. A gentle
and patient love is what you deserve.

Michael Tavon

**(*If You Struggle with Loving Yourself*)**

Remember this, there is someone who believes your
presence is the greatest gift in the world, and they look
forward to seeing you the moment they get out of bed. So
the next time you start a war with yourself by trying to
destroy all the beauty inside you. Think of them. Hopefully,
soon- you'll see what they see in you too.

## Overtime Lover

I know you've grown tired of
Giving full-time affection
to part-time lovers.
Constantly wasting time
trying to chase forever
in people who eventually disappear
you deserve to take a vacation
after working overtime
to find the perfect love,
it's time to give your heart a rest,
you deserve a break
so you can heal the brokenness
inside you
*the greatest love you'll ever find*
*is the love you'll unlock from within yourself*

Michael Tavon

## **Planting in Graves**

Going back to an ex
Is like trying to plant
Life in a grave

You'll find yourself trying to save
What's already dead,
There's no way to revive
A broken foundation
Why keep chasing
after what has long evaded,

Only heartbreak
awaits on the other side
A little hope still resides
In your mind
So you keep watering and planting

Until the dead soil Is soaked in your tears,
You refuse to move on
Because all the years You spent loving them

When the memories of yesterday
Were buried 6 feet deep
You were there with your sorrows
and a shovel, digging to retrieve
That old feeling again
Sadly, what you had
is gone

To Build a Home

But If you have the strength
To love the wrong person,
You possess the strength to move on,
Leave that grave alone
find a garden plant new love there

Michael Tavon

## **Thriving**

When life threw you stones
you created a mountain
When life tried to
drown you in tropical storms
You grew a rainforest
When you were presented with coal
You made diamonds under pressure
No matter what obstacles life presents
you find ways to survive and thrive

## **Oceans**

Empathy is like an ocean; you either drown or stay afloat, depending on how you swim through the waves of understanding. A deep understanding of perspectives outside your own will help you swim to shore. No need to be stubborn or closed-minded; you don't have to agree with every opinion, but please exercise kindness.

Michael Tavon

No matter how busy
Your days become
Never forget to make time
For yourself

## Leaving You

I'm sorry you had
to shed tears over me,
leaving you wasn't as easy
as I thought it would be

I wish heartbreak were simple
But it isn't
At the end of this war
You got hit in the crossfire

Maybe I was selfish for choosing myself
maybe I knew you deserved more peace
which meant less of me

Michael Tavon

## The Perfect Balance

There's nothing wrong with demanding excellence from
yourself but extend a hand of grace when you fall short.

And when you fall short, don't drown in a sea of self-pity;
life is about swimming through adversity to reach the shore
of fulfillment.

Once you reach the shore, celebrate your success but don't
let it get to your head. Remain grounded with your head
held high.

To Build a Home

Once you realize how special you are,
You'll stop giving those *voices of doubt* so much clout to
provide more space for your intuition to thrive.

Michael Tavon

## **<u>Smile Again</u>**

You could lose yourself
In yesterday's thoughts
Or find new life
In the memories waiting
To be made today
Are you ready to smile again?

The irony of life is so remarkable.
We are so distracted by our vanity needs
we ignore the fact

The most precious
and fragile things in life are intangible
and take them for granted

Michael Tavon

## A Poem Circa 2015

Life is so precious and often
taken for granted
It's the furthest thing from forever
Yet we treat it as if we have mulligans
We all ask the age-old questions
"Why am I here?"
"What's my purpose?"
We dedicate our whole existence
Trying to find those answers
But it's all so vague, often goes in vain
We work hard just to die
And be forgotten about
Most of us live with that fear
The fear of never finding that
Purpose, the fear of never creating a legacy,
the fear of never finding true happiness.
So we lose sleep,
dedicating each waking breath,
to attain those things,
For what? For us to die tomorrow,
next week, or some years down the road
Suddenly your hard work
Falls into an abyss that leads to nowhere.
Life is fragile, time ~ limited
And often unappreciated.

## Hello 2morrow

Many of us are reluctant to say goodbye to people, places, or things because we fear the unknown of a new tomorrow. I say, bury that fear over time; you'll gradually witness a new you emerging from the soil. You only get one chance to live in your present body, don't waste it on holding the past hostage. Tomorrow is eager to meet you, don't disappoint it by trying to water dead roots.

Michael Tavon

## Rebirth

Sometimes goodbyes
Can be as liberating as the first time
Air touches your soft skin
After living inside your mother's womb,

At first you may cry,
The pain may bruise,
Anxiety may travel down your spine,
But it's alright,

*Beyond all the fear*
There's a bright light telling you,
A new life is ahead
And a thousand hellos
are ready to meet you

To Build a Home

## The Apology, Your Inner Child, Deserves

I created so much distance between us
I no longer recognize you from the horizon
O how I reach for your silhouette
As you trot off into the distance

  My heart shatters when
  Your cry echoes amid the cool breeze
  I apologize for being a deadbeat
  You deserve so much better than me

Instead of protecting you
I left you in the dusk to fend
For yourself

  You try so hard to love me
  While I do everything to push you away
  I'm ashamed of who I've become,
  I don't want you to see me this way

Once I get my shit together,
I'll find my way back

  I hope you find it
  In that pure heart of yours
  To forgive me,
  Because I am deeply sorry
  For leaving you behind

Michael Tavon

**Use this page to write a message to your future self**

**Bonus Poems**

Michael Tavon

## Kill Us All

The Senate won't change a damn thing,
until they kill us all dead.
There's no code of ethics
for domestic terrorists with firearms.

They're so pro-life when the life
is in the womb
But don't give a shit
when a young life becomes a tomb

I guess this country loves guns
more than people
We were not created equal

Bloodshed, more children dead
Shots fired; grocery store turned red

Bullets fly like birds
While children flock for safety

They want us (the people) to be
numb and silent to violence

Inside my heart, there's a riot
Because there's nothing I can do
There's nothing we can do

To Build a Home

Tears of a nation, healing is a myth
Because our government believes
guns are more important
Than the innocent people who die

Michael Tavon

## **Let them Bullets Rain**

Another massacre, another massacre
Walls painted with the blood of innocent lives

The world doesn't stop
we've become so desensitized

Another one!?
But no one's surprised

We've been trained since the Columbine
Bullets fly high like birds on a summer day
Students duck for cover they can't find

So young, so pure
School is where they learn to die

The drills I remember so vividly
Lock the door - duck under the desk

Play hide n seek with the shooter
Don't expose your chest

What's going on,
A question Marvin Gaye
asked 50 years ago
The answer, we still don't know

Guns and drugs, we can buy
Off the corner

To Build a Home

But most can't afford
mental health coverage

How many children must pass away
Via bullet spray to inspire change?

"It's not a gun issue,
it's a mental health issue," they say

The way the folks in the White House
Protect guns over people is sickening
They show rage when a woman aborts
But do nothing when children
Turn into corpses

What's going on
We keep playing the same song

They tell us to vote,
For who exactly?

No one in the office gives a fuck
About our wants and needs

We're just commodities
for their greed.

In the land
where guns are valued
more than human life,
They only pretend to care
When we die

Michael Tavon

Reflection: This page is for you to jot down your thoughts
& feelings